Tales *of* Enchantment

Tales *of* Enchantment

Stories to Empower Positive Self-change

WENDY RILEY

BALBOA.
PRESS
A DIVISION OF HAY HOUSE

Balboa Press books may be ordered through booksellers or by contacting:

**158.
1**

Balboa Press
A Division of Hay House
1663 Liberty Drive
Bloomington, IN 47403
www.balboapress.com
1 (877) 407-4847

ISBN: 978-1-4525-1847-3 (e)
ISBN: 978-1-4525-1846-6 (sc)
ISBN: 978-1-4525-1848-0 (hc)

Library of Congress Control Number: 2014912309

Printed in the United States of America.

Balboa Press rev. date: 8/4/2014

To my husband, Graham, who has supported me
throughout this process and believed I could do this;
To my sons, Scott and Lee.
To my family and friends, I thank you all.

CONTENTS

INTRODUCTION

This book started as a hypnotherapy script book. I found that the books with stories available to support my hypnotherapy practice were quite limited. So I began to write my own stories. As a keen walker, I observed nature, trees, wildlife, and the river, and as I walked along the river through the woods, words would form in my mind and the essence of the stories would be formulated.

The scripts or stories not only represent my client's issues, but they also mirror my own journey of overcoming difficulties and challenges. I believe that self-belief, self-love, self-confidence, and self-worth are the foundation of being true to ourselves. Happiness comes from within, not from material possessions or through food, alcohol, or drugs. We need to fill the void within ourselves with positive thoughts and affirmations, so that we can believe in and love ourselves.

My stories have assisted many clients to make positive changes, and I felt that more people would benefit from these stories if

I changed it from a hypnotherapy script book to a self-help book. The unconscious mind is very receptive when we are relaxed. While we are reading, we become part of the story, thus allowing change to formulate and take place. This allows us to take on new ideas, thereby giving us new awareness of how we can be.

1

THE PATH

(Fear of letting go of what no longer benefits us and changing direction)

One day, a man decided to go to the zoo for the day. As he walked around the enclosures and observed the different animals, he came across an enclosure with a big brown bear and several smaller bears.

The big bear would walk from one side of the enclosure to the other. He went back and forth from one side to another, east to west, back and forth, west to east, all day, until nightfall, at which point he would go to his cave. It was here in his cave that he would dream and visualise what he really wanted and how he wanted to be. He knew he had an inner strength, an inner knowing, and an intuition, wisdom that could transform the way he was. He would lie in his cave, seeking the resources necessary for renewal and healing.

The bear would walk back and forth for hours, pacing along the same path from one side to the other, never changing his course. It was always on the same path, doing the same thing, day in and day out.

The bear was stuck. He knew he was stuck; his thoughts were keeping him in limbo. His thoughts represented or determined his feelings and behaviours. His thoughts were negative: They told him he couldn't move forward and that he wasn't good enough. He was worthless and useless, and he didn't deserve to be happy.

When he moved to the east, he felt that change was near. He would then go to the west, which showed him how to solve his problems, however he was frightened: He feared change. He feared moving from security, although dull and monotonous, to something new and unfamiliar. There was a part of him that wanted to change, and there was a part of him that wanted to stay stuck.

He longed to go swimming with the other bears in the pond at the top of the hill, where the other bears played happily in the water without a care in the world, jumping and splashing in the water and enjoying the coolness of the water out of the heat of the day's sun. He knew that when he growled at the other bears, it wasn't that he disliked them. Perhaps, though, it was because he was jealous of their being able to play without any concerns.

He wanted to be with them, doing the things that they were doing and being part of their world, however he was frightened. He longed for a day when he could be carefree and enjoy himself. He knew that the anger he felt for the others was actually anger towards himself. He was angry that he was unhappy and that he was unable to be who he really wished to be. He wished and desired to be carefree enough to socialise and be with the other bears.

One day when the bear was walking along his path, there was a thunderous bang. It was the loudest noise he had ever heard. This frightened him, and it made him jump and start to run up the hill. He stopped. He was no longer on the same old path: He was on a different path, and he started to look at his surroundings, for they were unfamiliar and strange.

He could see the old path he had walked every day back and forth, day in and day out. He no longer felt afraid to be on this part of the hill. In fact, he quite liked it. He could see so much more from that position. He felt more confident, stronger, and happier.

He could see the crowds of people who came to visit. He could see them laughing and having fun. He felt so much better about himself. He began to respect himself and change the way he thought about himself. He created positive thoughts and developed an attitude that he was good enough. He was worthy and useful, and he was happy.

Each day, the bear managed to move further and further up the hill until he reached the pond at the top, where the other bears were playing happily in the cool water. As he stood at the top of the hill, he started to wonder what he was so afraid of. He was now at the top of the hill, and he now knew his fears were completely unfounded.

He had allowed himself to let go of his old path and move forward onto a new path, one that made him feel alive.

The anxieties and worries that had kept him imprisoned were now gone. By letting go of the old, he was able to try new things. He then jumped into the cool water. He started to have fun with the other bears. He felt lighter, calm, relaxed, and free.

Like the flowing water, we must learn to go with the flow of life. It is through the challenges and difficulties that we realise we are at our most vulnerable. It is, however, when we are at our most vulnerable that we are in fact at our strongest. We can then understand that it is this darkness that encourages us and allows us to look inward to find light, courage, and love.

2

WISHING WELL

(To help increase self-belief, self-confidence, and self-esteem)

This is a story about a girl named Joy. She was out walking in the woods one beautiful autumn day. The trees were stunning with their array of colours. Some were red, others golden, and some of the leaves were still waiting to turn from green to orange or to whatever colour they were going to be. Joy took great delight in the many different colours and wondered at how clever nature was at adapting and transforming itself from one season to the next. She wished that she too could transform herself from the quiet, shy person she was with her many fears. She wished she were a confident person who believed in herself, her abilities, and her purpose in life. As she was pondering this, she came upon a wishing well.

This was no ordinary wishing well, for there were clear instructions on the wall of the well. The instructions said that anyone who wished to drink from this well had to dance around the well three times while saying the following:

I believe in myself
As I am worthy

I believe in myself
As I am fearless
I believe in myself
As I am in charge

Joy saw that once you have completed this rhyme three times, you must sit beside the well and imagine a huge cloud above your head. You must then release all your anxieties and fears until the cloud turns dark and ominous. Fill this cloud with all of your fears, worries, and anxieties. This cloud will then drift farther and farther away. The farther it goes, the lighter and more relaxed you will become. You will notice that things that would have bothered you in the past no longer have the same effect on you. You may then drink from the well.

So Joy began her dance around the well and chanted:

I believe in myself
As I am worthy
I believe in myself
As I am fearless
I believe in myself
As I am in charge
She repeated it for a second time:
I believe in myself
As I am worthy
I believe in myself
As I am fearless
I believe in myself
As I am in charge

The leaves began to swirl all around her. It was like a multicoloured coat of many colours. The reds, gold's, and yellows shimmered and twinkled in the autumn sunlight.

She began to laugh and feel free as she repeated the verse for the final time:

I believe in myself
As I am worthy
I believe in myself
As I am fearless
I believe in myself
As I am in charge

She then sat at the edge of the well, feeling safe, secure, and protected by her coat of many colours. She began to imagine that white fluffy cloud and began to release her misery and worries into it. She released her fear of not being good enough and of being shy and her lack of belief in herself. She released all the shame and guilt.

She released and let go. She forgave herself and accepted herself, and as she did this, she could see the cloud changing from white to grey to black. The cloud started to drift away into the sky. With it went all of her problems, worries, and unhappiness, never to return to her.

She then slowly lowered the bucket into the well until she heard a splash as it reached the bottom. She raised the bucket to the top, and some of the clear water splashed around the bucket and spilled onto the leaves on the ground. When the water landed on the leaves, they began to shimmer and shine as if by magic. Joy took a sip of water from the bucket, and she began to feel the magic of the water. She began to feel calm and free. She had an inner tranquillity and peacefulness that she had never experienced before. She felt safe, secure, and carefree.

THE TOWER

(Feeling trapped)

ow that you feel comfortable and relaxed, I want to tell you a story set within the grounds of a castle. I want you to think of a castle that you have visited, and I want to take you on a journey around this castle. This will be a magical and enlightening journey.

As you wander towards the entrance of the castle, you look up at the beautiful turrets, and you begin to wonder at the height and splendour of these structures.

I want you now to step inside the castle. We will go to the first room on the left. Go through the door into the room, and on the floor, you will see many rugs. When you look closer, you will see that these carpets are shimmering and moving on the floor and that they are all different colours and shapes. I want you to choose one. Choose one that draws your attention. Go right over to it, and touch it. As you touch that carpet, you realise that this is no ordinary carpet. Rather, it is one with such energy and enthusiasm that it draws you to it. Perhaps you are drawn to it because it's your favourite colour, or perhaps you are drawn to it because of the pattern and shapes on the carpet. It feels safe and secure, and it feels right.

This is no ordinary carpet; this is a magic carpet. The carpet is now inviting you to sit on it and explore the castle by allowing you to fly around the castle, over the roof tops that will allow you to see things more clearly and from a different angle. Imagine being able to view everything from down below or up above.

You are feeling so comfortable on your carpet and so relaxed that the carpet now feels part of who you are. To make the carpet move to the right or left or to stop or start it, all you have to do is think it.

As you sit on the carpet, it begins to move. The carpet moves slowly towards the window, and you drift through the window and out into a sunny spring day. The sun feels warm against your body, and you find yourself relaxing even deeper. You feel content and at peace. You have an inner knowing, and you know that change can start now or later today; you know that you may and will start to see things differently from now on.

The carpet begins to drift out into the castle's grounds and soar higher and higher towards the top of the castle. The wind whisks through your hair. As you become one with the carpet, you become one with yourself.

You now fly around the castle, going faster and faster until things begin to blend into one. The carpet slows when it comes to a tower on the east side of the castle. Beginnings always start in the east, since the sun rises in the east, and each day is a new day with a fresh beginning. It is the time of change. New ideas arise and awaken; change awakens. Spring is the season when all things begin to grow and awaken. The energy to flourish and develop begins here.

You are reminded of a story that you once heard about prisoners who had been imprisoned in that east tower. You hover on your carpet beside the window, peer through the iron bars, and begin to imagine what it would have been like to be imprisoned in that small tower.

The story went that many of the prisoners had been in that tower for ten or twenty years, and they had tried numerous ways to escape. They had tried to escape through the bars of the window, but the tower was so high that it was impossible. They would have fallen to their deaths if they had tried to make their escape this way.

They had tried to break down the walls of the tower to no avail. They had failed to escape. They had dreamed of being free and able to run around outside, enjoying nature and all that is. They imagined feeling the wind, sun, and rain on their faces, but they were trapped. Their frustration, isolation, and fear grew, and it made them feel hopeless, frustrated, and angry.

One day, a new prisoner arrived; he, too, looked for ways to escape, so that he could return to his simple, happy life. It was a life filled with love and security, a life of freedom. He asked the prisoners how they had tried to escape from this life, and they told him about their attempts to escape from the windows or to tunnel their way out.

The new prisoner went to the sturdy oak door and tried to open it while the other prisoners looked on in despair. They knew that it was hopeless; the only time that door ever opened was for someone new to arrive. Food and water were pushed through a hatch within the door. The new prisoner continued to examine the door, looking at the locks the handles, reviewing every part of the door. So instead of opening the door towards him, as all the other prisoners had done, he turned the handle and pushed the door in the opposite direction. The door opened. The door had never been locked. The prisoners had the ability all along to be free, simply by seeing things in an alternative way. The answers are always there, we simply have to remind ourselves to step back from the problem and see things in a different light. By shining a new clarity on something this allows us to move beyond our limitations.

As you hover on your carpet, you think about what has been trapping you or what have you imagined or thought that has been preventing you from moving forwards. What has been hindering you from escaping from this worry or trouble? There is always choice, and there are always solutions. A well-known therapist coined the phrase, "There are over 200 ways to wash dishes." There is always choice.

So take some time to think of new ways to resolve difficulties, worries, and anxieties with a new self-awareness of resources, experiences, and learnings that you may have overlooked. Be like the sun rising in the east. Perhaps by experiencing every day as a chance to learn, change, and grow, you can become what you most wish and desire.

THE SMOKE TRAIN

(The effects of smoking on the mind and body)

You're standing at the train station, waiting to embark on the next train, but this is no ordinary train. This is a special train. This train is an old-fashioned steam engine with three carriages. Which carriage will you choose? This train can go to the past, present, or future.

The first carriage is the one next to the engine, but there is nothing separating the carriage from the engine. The men in charge of stoking the fire are black from head to foot because the smoke and soot are bellowing throughout the carriage onto all the passengers. There is no door on the fire, and the men who have to stoke the fire are hot from the heat of the fire and black from the ash and soot. Their faces are black, and all that can be seen are the whites of their eyes.

The people in this carriage are all suffering from the effects of too much smoke; there are people coughing and clearing their throats. All the people struggle for breath. The heat is so intense, and this makes their breathing worse.

The people are all wheezing and gasping for breath in this carriage. Some could barely walk due to their breathing problems, and some are so thin because they don't have enough breath to eat. It was difficult to see who was there, but people could tell there were others by the sounds of their laboured breath. The wheezing that came from their lungs was raspy and forced.

The music being played in this carriage was "Every Breath I Take." Every breath is contaminated and putrid. With every breath, the air becomes more and more contaminated. This is all because they wanted to look cool and part of the in crowd back when they were teenagers. Whatever the reasons they had for starting, it no longer felt cool or fun. There was no fun anymore, and it most certainly wasn't cool. It felt dirty and smelly, and because it felt dirty and smelly, was it really that much fun?

In the second carriage, the people here are unsure of what they should do. Why should they change? They had glimpsed the future and seen what would happen if they continued on their present path. They now seen their health as a gift, and that gift is what they desired. They desired a carefree, healthy lifestyle because they wondered how it would now feel to be free from the burden of smoking. Because they longed for this, they realised that there is choice, and they choose to be a non-smoker.

The music that being piped in this carriage was "You Have No Desire to Smoke." You are now a non-smoker. Because you have no desire to smoke because you are a non-smoker, your body and mind will be pleased with the decision. Your body did not like and did not want that smoke, but you persisted. You felt dizzy wanting to cough because your body did not like that. Finally, your body accepted the fact. Smoking became part of your life, and later on when you tried to stop, you were unable to stop because your body did not know, and did not understand that you were stopping smoking. But your unconscious mind now understands that you have no desire to smoke since you are a non-smoker. Your body always wanted to be a non-smoker, and you will have no withdrawal symptoms at all.

In fact, your body will be pleased with your decision because it never enjoyed smoking. It knew how to enjoy life without smoking. Smoking means nothing to you. You will have no desire to smoke in the car, at home, or at work. You will have no desire to smoke outdoors or indoors because smoking means nothing to you. You are a non-smoker. You will have no desire to smoke despite, being around smokers, for you are now a non-smoker. When someone smokes around you, the smell of their smoke will make you feel sick and remind you that you are a non-smoker. You have no desire to smoke after a meal or first thing in the morning. You have no desire to smoke. You will not be substituting anything else for the smoking; you will also have better control over your other habits.

You will never smoke again because you are a non-smoker, and you will discover all the benefits from being a non-smoker, your health will improve, your mind will become clearer you will be financially better off, you will have extra money to do some of the things you have only ever dreamt of. You will be physically and mentally stronger as you will no longer be burdened with the need to smoke because you are a non-smoker. You have no desire to return to that life of smoking. Smoking made you feel dirty, smelly, and ill. Smoking controlled you, however now you control it.

In this third carriage, the air is clear, clean, and pleasant. The music being played in this carriage is "Breakaway." They are breaking away from the old ways of learning to take a chance, making their dreams, and desires become a reality. They are breaking away from the old and reaching out for the new. They have chosen to be a non-smoker, they had chosen their health, and they had chosen freedom.

The people in this carriage are healthy, hearty, and whole. They understand that their health is their wealth and that they have a choice in what they place in their bodies. Only they can make the changes they desire for they are in control of their destiny.

They have seen the past and into the future. The future showed their health floating away from them with every puff. Their health floated farther and farther away from them just because they wanted to be the same as everyone else. However, now they could choose to be who they wanted to be, and they could choose a healthier, better tomorrow.

So what carriage will you choose? Do you choose the carriage of the future, the past, or the present? The present is a gift of clean air and a healthier you. Choose **now** to be a non-smoker.

CHOCOLATE GODDESS

(Filling a void with sweetness)

This is a story about a chocolate goddess named Kitty. She was over six feet tall. She had long blonde hair and was made entirely of milk chocolate. She looked and tasted delicious. Everyone loved Kitty; she was so popular. She was much loved, very much wanted, and highly sought after. People found themselves spending more and more time with Kitty, and more and more of their days thinking about Kitty. There was a reason for this: She made people feel fantastic. She made them feel alive, because she released natural endorphins that caused people to feel euphoric around her. When she released these natural endorphins, people no longer felt frustrated, depressed, or agitated. They became relaxed and happy, wrapped in a feeling of contentment and bliss. They were smothered in the love she gave them.

However, there was a side effect: They needed more and more of this chocolate to induce the same feelings and emotions. The people were beginning to notice that they were gaining weight. Their clothes no longer fitted them, and they felt bloated and sluggish. It was controlling their lives.

There was lots of speculation as to what Kitty may be made of: Would her tummy be full of soft chocolate or nougat or jelly?

It made people's mouths water just thinking about it. One day, when lots of people were all gathered around her she began to laugh, and something peculiar began to happen. She laughed so hard that her stomach began to break and an opening began to appear. As her stomach began to separate and unfold, everyone leaned closer, expecting to see at long last what was inside the goddess. People expected the goddess to be even more exquisite in the inside as she was on the outside.

However, this beautiful goddess was hollow inside; there was emptiness, sadness, a hunger, a void. As she looked down and saw that emptiness within her, she began to weep.

Her tears spoke of pain, disappointment, and frustration. She began to grieve her losses, and she cried for the lack of sweetness in her life. It was the lack of joy, security, and heartbreak and the loss of what she so dearly wanted.

She was hungry inside for love and joy, and as she cried, she allowed herself to let go of her pain. She let go of the past and the pain, accepted and forgave herself. She accepted herself and forgave herself knowing that lessons had been learned and this in turn allowed change to take place. As she forgave herself, she began to feel more love. Because she felt more love, she felt more fulfilled, more complete, and more wonderful.

By releasing the old stale ways of being, new ways of being began to fill her being. As she began and continued to have a new self-awareness of what she desired, she realised that she was both powerful and desirable. She was proud to be the woman she was because she loved herself and felt self-fulfilled.

As she released the past, the void within her began to fill with love and understanding, allowing the emptiness to be filled with joy, laughter, fun, and hope. Her thoughts were of love and joy, and because her thoughts were filled with love and joy, so were her actions and her feelings. This gave her a greater feeling of safety, security, and belief. She now chose to love and accept herself, releasing her own natural feel-good endorphins.

THE HEALTHY HORSE

(Overeating)

This is a story about a horse. He was a beautiful horse. He was brown with white markings on his face. He had a gorgeous mane of brown hair and a long swishing tail. He lived with his family in a stunning field overlooking a river and was cared for by the kind farmer.

He was an adult horse, but when he was younger, he came upon by accident at the very bottom of the field along a narrow grassy lane. He found where the farmer would discard any extra food from the house. Being young and inquisitive, he sniffed the air around him, unsure whether he should try the food there. He was fed well by the farmer, and there was ample fresh grass in the field. Knowing this and feeling relaxed, comfortable, and well-nourished, he about turned, sniffing the air and travelled back along the grassy lane round one corner and then the second corner and returned back to his family, who were contentedly grazing in the field.

Several years later, something happened, although he wasn't sure entirely what. Something had changed. He felt more restless, constantly wandering around the field. He couldn't concentrate on anything, and he was bored and tired. And then one day, he found himself returning to that same grassy lane round one corner and then another.

This time, he felt so different. Because he felt different, he did more than just sniff the air. When he sniffed the air, he began to look at the food left by the farmer. He began to salivate with the thought of that tempting food lying there. There were vegetables, carrots, turnips, and potato peelings, as well as crisps, biscuits, and chocolate.

He looked at the food, and because something had changed, that something was making him feel different. He had no idea what. He began to sample the food that had been left by the farmer. There was so much food. When he first tried these things, he found that he didn't really like what he was eating. The chocolate was too sweet. The crisps were hard and tangy. He persevered, though, until he started to really enjoy them. He knew that these foods weren't good for him; he knew he shouldn't be eating them. He knew that this was his guilty secret, and he did feel guilty. The difficulty was that when he started eating he found that he couldn't stop until it was all gone. He wanted to stop, however he found it increasingly difficult to stop once he started. The more he ate, the more he wanted to eat. He didn't want to eat it, but something deep within was making him want to eat.

There was a frustration about it all: It was a frustration that he needed to eat this, as well as a frustration of when all the food was gone. He was also beginning to notice that his physical health was beginning to suffer; he felt tired and sluggish, and this was due to the extra burden and stress he was carrying.

Every day, he would venture along the grassy lane around one corner and then the other; sometimes, he found himself doing this more than once a day. He couldn't help himself he had to do it. There was a part of him that enjoyed this, and there was another part that disliked what he was doing to himself. He couldn't understand it. He didn't want to do this, but he couldn't stop himself either.

He would often think back to when he was young and how this had never been a problem for him before. He had physical strength and vitality, and also the emotional ability to go on in life. He began to ask himself what resources he needed to recognise the difficult issues that were causing him to behave in this way. What had changed? And what did he need to help him overcome this? He stood there on the hillside, pondering this question watching the river.

He looked down at the river and watched it as it slowly meandered. It always flowed, never stopping. If there were any obstacles it came across, it didn't stop and worry. It simply moved around any obstacles in its way. The river never doubted itself, knowing that it could and would overcome any difficulties. The river had a knowing that there was always a way around any difficulties or challenges.

So the horse contemplated his own problems and looked for new ways to overcome his own personal difficulties. Knowing that there is always a way, and because he had a new self-awareness, knowledge, and understandings, he was able to overcome his own obstacles. He found new beneficial ways to nourish his body and mind. He chose to fuel his body with foods that were hearty and nutritious because he deserved to treat his body and mind with respect. When he found himself restless and bored, his mind found ways to distract him from thinking about food. Every day and in every way, he found that things were more relaxed, carefree, and comfortable, and this reminded him of the way things used to be and what he now desired.

THE DUCK THAT THOUGHT SHE COULDN'T FLY

(A fear of flying and releasing old patterns and behaviours)

This is a story about a beautiful, clever, intelligent female mallard duck. She had a mainly brown body and an orange bill. She lived on the local river with her brothers and sisters and her mother. They enjoyed swimming. They skimmed the water effortlessly, gliding eloquently on the river and enjoying the way the water lapped against their bodies. The ducklings felt so safe and secure, following their mother wherever she went, feeling protected and free. They ducked and dived for the many plants and insects that lived within the river that their mother had shown them how to find safely and easily. She had also shown them how to go onto the river bank to search for food: acorns, seeds, and berries. She had shown them how to care for the beautiful feathers and how to preen and clean themselves while in and out of the river.

Now it was time for them to learn the final skill they needed to be independent. The ducklings needed to learn to fly. So mother duck demonstrated how they had to glide faster and faster along the river, gaining speed and momentum. They used their strong muscles within their bodies to flap their wings, pushing their wings downwards, pushing air downwards, thus generating the lift and thrust required to make them airborne. It was time to learn the skill needed to be free.

So the duckling began to glide faster and faster along the river, preparing to take off. Seeing that her brothers, sisters, and mother began to soar higher and higher into the sky, she began to quack in a high-pitched tone. She found herself unable to do what the others had done so successfully, without fear, panic, or dread. She continued to skim along the water, quacking and quacking, feeling more and more alarmed with every second that passed. What was stopping her from doing this natural, everyday movement? What fears was she holding onto? What emotions and feelings was she side-stepping or ignoring?

What was it she needed to release to accomplish a new way of being?

The mother duck returned asking the same questions: What was stopping her from doing this natural, everyday movement? What fears was she holding onto? What emotions and feelings was she side-stepping or ignoring?

What was it she needed to release to accomplish a new way of being?

The mother duck went onto explain about how mankind had watched birds fly and wondered how they did it, wondering also if they too could fly. Only after studying birds were they able to build machines that could fly through the air safely, easily, and quickly.

So the mother duck reminded her daughter that we sometimes need to return to the parts of ourselves that need to feel safe and comfortable. It is necessary to filter out what is not needed, decide what is important, and discover what is true. Take a few moments to think about what is no longer needed or what can be discarded. Then choose or notice what is meaningful and true.

All you need to master is how to manoeuvre through the waters of life with grace, showing emotional comfort and protection. By doing this, you will discover how to move with ease and comfort in all your actions, emotions, and thoughts. This will then allow speedy movements for ideas to take flight, teaching us to be calm and graceful when handling our emotions.

So she tried once more to learn the skill to free herself from the river and to be independent. The mother duck demonstrated how she had to glide faster and faster along the river to gain speed and momentum. Using the strong muscles in their bodies to flap their wings, they pushed their wings downwards, pushed air downwards, and generated the lift and thrust required to make them airborne. Using her inner strength, love, and security for herself, she allowed old patterns, behaviours, people, and situations from the past to be healed, giving her the freedom to soar in new ways and directions.

Trusting herself and believing, she began to feel lighter as she rose into the air, gliding and soaring effortlessly over the river and trees. So by journeying within she had discovered how to set herself free and travel to new horizons.

8

THE SALMON

(Coping with daily struggles and worries)

As the man stood at the edge of the river, he watched as the river flowed slowly past. The dark waters moved silently and continually along its way, always finding a way around any difficulties it may encounter. He often stood watching the river, time passing like the river, slowly and continually.

As he stood, a salmon jumped out of the water, its silver belly glistening in the late summer's night. He contemplated the salmon making its leap of faith from the deep, dark waters into the light.

It made him think about what the salmon's aim was? Is the salmon's aim to overcome all obstacles that may present themselves? Perhaps its aim is to be reunited with all that is: the cycle of life.

At first glance, the man thought that it looked like the salmon was troubled. In reality, though, the salmon only appears to be struggling as it moves upstream. The salmon was not really fighting the currents, it was jumping to go deeper so that it could ride the reverse currents below the surface, so that the currents could gracefully carry it upstream.

It made him contemplate what someone once taught him about the word *somersault*. It was inspired by the salmon leaping. The word *somersault*, in fact, stems from the word *salmon* (sault). Somersaulting children are being playful and nimble. Being able to be childlike is yet another lesson to be learned from salmon. I wonder how that would be or feel to be living in the moment without fear or worry.

The man thought that this was a beautiful metaphor for life. At the surface, there is much that appears to be a struggle. There are an abundance of issues we deal with every day, such as work, family, finances, and health. When we allow ourselves to delve deeper and go below the surface, the energy and wisdom we need to flow through life is uncovered. It was there all along, but as we jump and dive deeper, we are then able to connect with those energies.

We can learn from the salmon: how to leap with joy in anticipation at the prospect of a new day and also to know that no matter where we are, we are always on our way home. Being light-hearted, open, innocent, and childlike is not the aid to reaching the goal. Rather, it is the goal itself. As you delve into the currents below have fun in learning to roll with the currents beneath the surface and allow the wisdom to flow.

That feeling of peace makes you realise how you are changing. As your new self-awareness increases, you will become aware of those things you can use as you use more of yourself. These are teachings, abilities, and skills you may have overlooked before to give you new ways of thinking and doing things. Because you allow yourself to find the answers that you need, you can utilise this to become the person you so desire to be. Delve deep and go below the surface to discover what wisdom and energies await you.

HARMONY ISLAND

(Dealing with anger, hurt, and disappointment)

This is a story about two giants who lived on the island of Harmony. Their names were Hope and Faith, and they had lived together for a long time on this island. It was a beautiful island, and everything was very peaceful and calm. The waves would lap against the sandy beach gently and quietly. The birds sang all day; their tunes were beautiful and exquisite. The trees floated in the wind in time to the melody the birds sang. The sun shone every day, bringing warmth and happiness. It was a wonderful place to be.

The two giants had been friends for years, and on this particular day, they had found a beautiful shell in the sea that glowed different colours in the sunshine. They picked it up out of the water and declared that it would look lovely as a necklace. This is when things became difficult: They both wanted it, saying that one had seen the shell before the other. They began to argue about who it belonged to. Because the island had not experienced anything like this before, things began to change. The sun went behind a cloud, and the cloud became bigger and blacker. The wind blew and blew, and the calm sea began to produce angry waves that started to crash onto the beach. These waves became larger and larger.

The more the giants argued, the colder the day became. The waves swept higher and higher up onto the beach, until the two giants had to pull on their socks and shoes before a massive wave completely covered the beach. The huge wave swept away the shell. The giants ran as fast as they could away from the beach and up into the mountains. As they ran, they continued to argue.

They now found themselves on an island that was dark and cold. The birds no longer sang; they appeared sad and frustrated that they could no longer sing and be happy. The waves from the sea were angry and swollen. The waves had destroyed the island, leaving only two small mountains surrounded by water. The giants now found themselves living on top of one of the small mountains in the middle of the sea. They continued to shout and argue to each other from their respective homes.

Their anger grew as they found new ways to mistreat each other; they began to throw rocks at each other. The rocks and insults would stop when it was bedtime; this was a time for them to reflect on their anger and what this meant to them. They were both very unhappy. They missed having fun and laughing. They felt guilty that the sun no longer shone and the birds were soundless. However, both were stubborn, and neither wished to apologise and forgive.

This night, Faith thought she would creep up to Hope's mountain and push her off her mountain into the sea while she slept. So she crept as quietly as a giant can up towards Hope's mountain; however, just before she got to the top of the mountain, Faith awoke. They looked at each other from top to toe, and instead of being angry, they started to laugh. And they laughed and laughed.

The reason they started to laugh was because when the waves had become higher and higher on the day they started to argue. And it was only now that they realised they were wearing different coloured shoes. Faith was wearing one pink and black shoe, and her other shoe was a green yellow and black shoe. Hope was wearing the same. They could see that they were both now wearing odd shoes, and this would start them off laughing again.

As they laughed, things began to change. The sun came out from behind the clouds, the wind stopped blowing, and the sea began to recede. The more they laughed, the island of Harmony began to reappear. The flowers grew where water had once been, and the birds sang their lovely melodies once more. The giants were friends once again, and they noticed that this feeling of peace makes you realise how you are changing.

So now when they find a shell, they place it to their ears, but not just to hear the sounds of the ocean. Shells are very powerful tools of transformation, giving animals camouflage, security, and protection. The giants knew that each shell was created as a home by an individual animal to provide safety and shelter. The giants now had awareness that shells bring important messages about emotions and how it is important to be kind to yourself and laugh at yourself and with others.

Both giants now wore a shell necklace to remind them of the importance of friendship and happiness. To live on the island of Harmony, everyone needed to live in a state of kindness, joy, hope, and harmony.

10
MRS ALLSORTS

(Embracing the new and letting go of the old)

Have you ever opened a bag of liquorice allsorts? What a sight to behold: all the different colours, shapes, and sizes. The colours, the smell, and the memory of how these sweets taste and feel all add to this lovely, mouth-watering experience.

People are like a bag of allsorts; we are all different. We are different colours, shapes, and sizes. And it's okay to be different: it is safe, and it is fun. Different is special and remarkable. Here is a story about an extraordinary woman called Mrs Allsorts.

Mrs Allsorts lived in a village where she was well-known. She was a kind, helpful, wise, and lovely woman. She had quite a hard life, with many traumas to endure, and this could be reflected in the clothes she wore. When she felt that life was treating her fairly and she was feeling positive about herself, she would be clothed from top to toe in pink. She would wear a pink floppy hat that would sit on top of her head, showing off her beautiful smiling face. There was a gorgeous pink top and a skirt and shoes to match. When she moved along the village, she appeared to float as she glided to her destination. People would stop to admire this amazing woman as her positive, invigorating energy touched anyone she came in contact with. The love she had for herself and for all around her was delightful.

However, when she was feeling low and listening to her inner critic, that inner voice called the ego who loves us to live in fear and worry, she would begin to dwell on her past hardships. Her past hardships were many, and when she thought about this, she felt broken. She felt damaged or faulty and in need of repair. When she felt like this, she would wear black clothes. She felt dark and hopeless, burdened by the past. So her clothes would reflect this feeling of darkness and gloom, mirroring how she was feeling at this time. Her walking mirrored this feeling, and she walked slowly as if her feet had to be pulled through mud. Each step was painfully slow as she journeyed on her way.

This day, while out walking, Mrs Allsorts was dressed in black. She met a young boy, and he asked her, "What is making you look so sad?"

She replied, "I am not sad."

The boy replied, "You look sad. If you're not sad, then it must be your clothes that you are wearing that are sad."

Mrs Allsorts looked down at her clothes, and she became aware that she did indeed look broken hearted. She looked sad and burdened. The boy went on to say that when she removed her clothes and shoes when she went home that night, she was to let go or forgive herself of the sadness, guilt, anger, pain, disappointment, and anything else she was still holding onto from the past. With every piece of clothing she removed, she was to let go of the darkness of the past.

So that night just before removing her dark clothes, she remembered what the boy had said. As she removed each item of clothing, she let go of the feelings of sadness, guilt, anger, pain, disappointment, and anything else she was still holding onto from the past. She removed her black shoes and threw them across the room, for they represented her need to run away from her feelings. Next came the black skirt and tights. She also threw them across the room, for they portrayed a covering up of her insecurities and her perceived failings. Then she removed her blouse and her hat and the feelings of fear and the need for protection, and these too were thrown across the room. She now had a pile of clothes in the middle of the floor. She was bare. She had bared her soul.

This is when we are at our most vulnerable, and this is also when we are at our strongest and most powerful. We can take control of and change what no longer fulfils and helps us. With this inner strength and power, she let go of all the sadness, guilt, anger, pain, disappointment, and anything else she was still holding onto from the past.

As she looked at the pile of clothes, she felt lighter, carefree, happy and joyful. So she gathered up her clothes, and she took them to her fire in the living room. She placed them in the flames. As she watched the flames flicker orange and red, she allowed her old feelings to be undone by the light. She watched the darkness move into the light and she began to hum a tune:

I am at peace with my own feelings. I am safe where I am. I create my own security. I love and approve of myself.

She repeated this mantra: "I am at peace with my own feelings. I am safe where I am. I create my own security. I love and approve of myself."

From that day on, she wore less and less black. And because she was wearing less and less black, she found herself wearing all the colours of the rainbow, but especially pink. This was why she became known as Mrs Allsorts.

11

THE SPINNING PLATES

(Stress, insomnia, and getting life in balance)

This is a story about a man. This man is an intelligent, kind, family man who worked hard as a professional. In his spare time, he had a hobby. His hobby was to spin plates. He balanced his plates upon bamboo canes and touched them gently to start them moving. As they began to move faster and faster, the plates would begin to sing a beautiful tune or melody. The different plates would then harmonise with one another, creating beautiful music. He spun the plates for those people in his family who were most important to him. So he spun a plate for his mother, father, each of his three children, his wife, and himself. There were seven plates in total.

His aim was to ensure that all of these plates spun easily and that they were balanced upon the bamboo canes.

He began this hobby ten years ago, first for his elderly parents, then his teenage children, and then for his wife and for himself. These plates required regular attention, and a lot of time and effort necessary to make this happen. Sometimes, the plates would expectantly slow down, and he would have to rush from one plate to another to ensure that they didn't fall and break.

When the plates slowed, the music slowed. The tune that was being played changed, and the notes no longer sounded so clear or balanced. The notes sounded frightened and muddled and they were no longer in tune with the moment, but worrying about what would happen in the future or living in the past. He thought that something terrible was about to happen, causing everything to tumble around his feet.

He was finding that he was spending more and more time ensuring that his plates spun smoothly. He found himself spending more and more time away from doing things for himself. He could have perhaps used this time differently. The more time he spent on spinning the family members' plates, the more he had neglected his own plate. It was becoming slower and slower.

Now realising that he was in fact overlooking his own plate, he decided that the only choice he had to look after these spinning plates properly was to reduce the amount of sleep he had, so that he could give this his full undivided attention. He would go to bed at the same time every night; however, he started awakening early in the morning to do what he needed to do.

The more he worried about what he needed to do, the more fearful he would become. He felt stifled. He needed to let go of what no longer benefited him and do what he wanted to do. It was hard work trying to juggle all of these different plates for all of these different people. The lack of sleep was causing him to feel tired and lethargic. He was unable to concentrate properly, unable to do not only what he wanted to do but also what he ought to be able to do.

All he really wanted to do was to release the old and welcome the new into his life. He decided that he needed to let go of his fears and trust the process of life. So he stopped spinning the many different plates, and he concentrated on his own plate.

He allowed himself to create a new life that completely supported him. He moved beyond his old limitations and allowed himself to express freely and creatively what supported him. He found that by doing this, his own plate began to spin freely and with ease, creating new melodies that totally supported him. He felt safe and secure. Because he felt safe and secure, he was able to slip into peaceful sleep, knowing that tomorrow would take care of itself. By learning to take care of his own needs first, seeing this as being self-fulfilling and not selfish, he was able then to contribute to his family in a far more beneficial, supporting, and pleasing way.

12

THE FAIRY CAKE BAKER

(To increase confidence and self-belief)

This is a story about a lady who loved baking. Her name was Jolene, and she was a lovely, kind, and strong woman who found that baking helped her to relax. Time passed in a flash when she was baking. She loved that when you put different ingredients together, they produced amazing beautiful smells and created something entirely new.

Jolene knew how to bake because her grandmother had taught her. She had taught her how to take ingredients, and with a little love and patience, create whatever she wished. One of Jolene's favourite things to make was fairy cakes or cupcakes. She would decorate them with beautiful icing, creating different designs for each one. Because she was passionate about what she did, the cakes appeared to bubble and burst as they rose from their small beginnings into tall prominent towers, climbing and rising out of their humble beginnings, growing into strong hearty cakes.

So it came as a bit of an upset the day Jolene tried to make lemon soufflés. She got the eggs, castor sugar, lemons, double cream, gelatine, and almonds. She put the yolks of the eggs and the lemon juice and zest into a bowl. She stood over a pan of simmering water and whisked until the custard mixture was thick. She added the gelatine and folded in the egg whites and cream into the custard mixture with light movements until everything was mixed together. And then she placed the soufflés into the oven to bake in their individual ramekin dishes.

It was when she went to remove the soufflés from the oven that she found that they were flat and unresponsive. The soufflés had not risen; they were smooth and lifeless. *So* Jolene tried again to make the soufflés, for she wasn't someone who gave up easily. She was strong in character, and it was this strength that had seen her through her many difficulties. So she tried again, and on the third attempt, she started to cry with frustration as to why this soufflé would not rise. What was causing this cake not to transform or change into the cake she knew it could become? As she cried, she asked for help and guidance.

In the next moment, there was a puff of flour. The room sparkled and shimmered, and Jolene realised that her fairy godmother stood alongside her and asked how she could help. Jolene explained the problem with the soufflés and how no matter what she did, they didn't seem to soar and rise to what they should be.

"Aaaaaaah," said the fairy godmother. "I will show you how to make your cakes rise." So she put the ingredients into the bowl and asked Jolene to do the same. She started to whisk the ingredients together, and when she did this, tiny bubbles floated all around her, tickling her nose and making her laugh.

Jolene tried but only managed one small bubble and looked despondently at her fairy godmother.

Try again, but this time, believe that you can do this. See what happens. So Jolene fluffed up the ingredients, and this time, two more bubbles appeared around her.

The fairy godmother said, "When you whisk, you must tell yourself you believe and that you are worthy of this, and everything else in your life."

So Jolene once again whisked the soufflé ingredients, and more bubbles appeared. The fairy godmother laughed and said, "You are nearly there; there are more ingredients you must add: belief, self-worth, self-approval, and the most important one of all is love. When we love ourselves, all fear is expelled. When fear is ousted, it allows room for the growth of new ways of being and doing."

Jolene added the extra ingredients into her soufflés; belief, self-worth, self-approval, and love. There were bubbles everywhere. Some were heart-shaped, some were round, but they were there in abundance. They tickled Jolene's nose and ears, making her laugh and feel light and happy. She was surrounded by bubbles, making her feel lighter and more carefree than she had felt for a long, long time. She placed her soufflés into the oven, and when she returned, twenty minutes later the soufflés were the lightest, liveliest and brightest she had ever seen. As she gazed in wonder at this amazing sight, she realised that she had the potential to create all that she desired because she believed she could.

MR MOON AND MRS SLEEP

(Understanding sleep)

This is a story about the moon, and a woman who has difficulty sleeping. This woman has had difficulty sleeping for many many years, and tonight, she was looking out her bedroom window at the moon, which was a waning crescent. She gazed up at the moon, knowing that it went through its own special cycles. As she watched the crescent moon glowing in the starry sky, she realised how dark everything would be without the light from the stars and moon.

The moon appeared to be whispering to her, asking her why she was staring up at him when she should be asleep in bed. Although he knew he was a wondrous sight to behold, he was also aware of the vital role sleep played in maintaining good health and well-being. Getting enough quality sleep at the right times can help protect your mental health, physical health, quality of life, and safety. When we sleep, our bodies heal and repair themselves.

So the moon asked the lady what was troubling her that she needed to gaze at him. She explained that she could get off to sleep, but then she would awaken in the middle of the night and then she would be unable to get back to sleep again. Her mind would re-create all of her worries and difficulties, and it would also create future doubts and concerns. These worries in her mind caused her more suffering and anguish. Because of these uncertainties, she lay awake at night. The more she worried about not sleeping, the more exhausted she became. She found herself weary and drained. Her health had become affected, and she had found herself feeling very stressed and frazzled indeed.

So the moon said, "I want you to go back to bed and do some slow breathing. Count to four in an in breath and four in an out breath for several minutes, allowing your mind to concentrate upon your breathing. Then imagine watching a river moving slowly as it meanders gently past, observing how it flows in one direction just going with the flow. As you continue to imagine that river moving slowly, so slowly, observing how it flows. It flows in one direction. A river never worries about what is in front of it or what has gone behind it. It just thinks about the now, the present moment.

As you imagine this river and all the qualities a river has, you will repeat to yourself the following three times:

I lovingly release the day and slip into peaceful sleep, knowing tomorrow will take care of itself. I allow myself to sleep easily.

I lovingly release the day and slip into peaceful sleep, knowing tomorrow will take care of itself. I allow myself to sleep easily.

I lovingly release the day and slip into peaceful sleep, knowing tomorrow will take care of itself. I allow myself to sleep easily.

As you do this, you will find yourself drifting along that river, flowing with the current and allowing yourself to drift into a peaceful, tranquil sleep, perhaps dreaming, and then floating into a deeper restful and healing sleep. When you awaken in the morning, you will feel, refreshed, revitalised, and relaxed because you now know that tomorrow will take care of itself.

So the woman strove to do this every night, and just as the moon had suggested, she found herself sleeping better and better with every night that passed. She now knew that tomorrow would take care of itself.

14

THE WARRIOR OF LIGHT

(For people who feel they just don't fit in)

The room was dark and full of what he thought was mannequins, all faceless and all the same. The men were dressed in jeans and checked shirts, while the women were dressed in dark skirts and white blouses. In the corner of the room, there was a sink and a tap that dripped continuously. On closer inspection, the dripping tap was dripping extremely slowly. After watching for several minutes, he noticed that it took lots of drips to cover the bottom of the white basin.

Meanwhile, the mannequins began to move around the room. He then realised that these were humans who all looked the same, spoke the same, dressed the same, and behaved the same. They were like clones, all living an identical existence. He felt like an outsider; he felt disconnected from these people. His tastes in television were different; he had a diverse choice in music that made him unique and unusual. This made him feel socially isolated and awkward.

There were some who shared his alternative views and pleasures, and this made him feel worthwhile and complete. His main passion was for electronic music; the beats caused the energy to pulsate through his body, making him feel alive and complete. This completeness made him feel connected and a kinship for life.

He consistently tried to involve these people in his taste for music. However, after several minutes, he would give up, knowing that there was no connection. And because there was no connection, he would disengage from them feeling alienated and lonely.

As he watched the dark humans move around the room, he could see that some of them were slightly lighter in colour than the others, and as he looked closer, he could see that these were some of the people who had listened to what he had to say about his passions.

The sound of the dripping of the tap caught his attention. He approached the sink and emptied out the water that was in the basin. He observed the tap slowly dripping, dripping, dripping into the empty basin. With patience and persistency, the slowly dripping tap began to fill the bottom of the basin. It took a long time to cover the bottom of the basin, and when this had occurred, the next drip would come and then the next. More and more of the basin would be covered with water.

It made the man think about his interactions with these people and how after he tried for only a short while when relating with them that he had given up. If he became like the dripping tap and gradually and gently nurtured them with information, they would begin to develop an awareness. He now had an understanding that he had to accept their beliefs and values. No one needed to change or become anything that did not wish to be.

He understood that this challenge was not thinking less of himself or by putting himself either above or below others; he was no more significant than anyone else. He was learning to be flexible and adapt rather than standing tall, full of pride and self-importance. It was necessary for him to accept other people's views and opinions in order to be open-minded, kind, and considerate. He put aside his need to be heard, so that the bright light of what he was presenting to these people could begin to shine.

He decided to be like the dripping tap and filter his wisdom by talking to them about his interests and encouraging them to open up and try something different. Ever so slowly, more and more people began to listen as he trickled knowledge and new teachings. As they accepted this, the darkness left and the light appeared. The man found that the more he danced to life's new experiences, the more enjoyment he received. So he found himself dancing more and more to the beat and rhythm of his own internal music, the music of love and understanding.

MUD HUTS

(Melting away those old self-limiting beliefs)

It's a beautiful sunny spring afternoon, and you're out walking in nature when you stumble upon a building which is round in structure. This building has a roof and many circular walls. It is made of clay soil mixed with water until it had become thick and left to dry. The roof is thatched and made of grass. It had been here for many, many years, and it has proven to be made of tough and lasting material.

There is a small door, and you decide to enter, and there is a note that says:

Break down these walls that you have created.

Destroy those walls that no longer serve your highest good.

What barriers have you constructed that are holding you back?

See these mud walls as your walls and see them as your limitations, so knock down these walls now and set yourself free. On the ground you will find an axe. Use this to erase those walls and beliefs you have produced that no longer benefit you.

You pick up the axe, and you raise it above your shoulder. You swing at the mud walls, and you have made a small mark or indentation on the wall. You swing again, and this time there is a weakening and the wall starts to disintegrate. You continue to hit the walls until the first wall has been reduced to rubble. This rubble of earth can no longer support itself. This dirt, this mess, has no place in your life. And as you look down, you can see these walls for what they really are. They are beliefs or thoughts that no longer benefit you. Take a minute (or what feels like a minute) to think about what beliefs you have just removed or cleared. What did you believe about yourself that was anything but truthful?

As you continue to contemplate that, you then notice another wall with a note on it. This message reads:

Well done, well done. You have removed the first obstacles in your path.

Knock down this wall, and you will find yourself even closer to discovering your heart's desire.

At your feet, you will find a candle and a match so that you can see where you need to go in the fading light.

As you light the candle and the flame flickers a short distance in front, it is only enough for you to see the wall that's visible before you. You raise your axe and begin to strike the wall. Soon, this wall is also rubble around your feet. These hindrances that have held you back are now gone. You feel lighter, you feel happier, and you feel free.

There is one final wall with one final message. This message says:

Well done, well done. You are nearly there, one last wall to destroy.

In the centre of this structure, you will find your heart's desire.

At your feet, you will find a torch to help you on your journey.

You pick up the torch, and you shine it on the wall. The torch brightly illuminates what is all around, and you can now see things in a new perspective.

You have now created a willingness to experience something, to be shown something, and to receive more of something. Because you can see all that's there, you can now see that there is a door on this wall. You now see new solutions, new ways of being and doing, and new choices. You open the door, and the wall that surrounded this falls to the earth.

You see what you so desire. That clearing has allowed a new space and a new energy to be revealed because you have connected with your true self, your inner self, the real you. All that was holding you back has been removed and released, and you can recognise that whatever your heart desires will become your destiny. So visualise what you so desire. See it: What does it look like? Feel it: What emotions will be attached (excitement, happiness, love, worthiness, accomplishment)? Hear it: What thoughts do you hear, what praise do you give yourself, and what compliments do your friends and family give you? See, feel, and hear your heart's desire, and it will be.

THE BEAR
NECESSITIES

(Anxiety, worry, stress, and the need to let things go)

This is a story about a bear who lives in the beautiful Canadian countryside. This bear had lived there for a long time, and he was now an adult bear. His mother and father had also stayed in this area, and he found this place to be very safe and familiar. He loved the beautiful trees, the vibrant colours of the leaves, and the beauty of the plants and flowers.

Although he knew this habitat well, he was finding himself to be more and more anxious about things that never used to bother him. These were things like going places and meeting other bears. He seemed to be fine with his own immediate family, but he considered anyone else difficult to deal with. He had sought guidance during the long months in hibernation, where he had reflected and pondered on his emotions and thoughts. He knew that his strengths were within him and that he needed to trust and follow his instincts to move forward.

He was beginning to find that these situations where he was in the company of others, made him feel hot and sweaty. This then started to make him breathe rapidly. He then would begin to think that something terrible was about to happen, and because of this, he started to get pains in his tummy and other symptoms. Sometimes, he got pain and wind in his tummy when he wasn't even meeting anyone but was just getting ready to go about his day. When the wind and pain got real bad, he found himself doubled up, rolling on his side, or massaging the sore area to get rid of the pain.

Because the pain was so debilitating, he found he could no longer do the things he wanted to do. When the pain subsided, he needed to go to the toilet frequently, which was a source of embarrassment. He thought that everyone was watching and staring as he ran back and forth to relieve himself. He felt drained and tired and just wanted to rest. He felt trapped just like the wind that was within him. He felt powerless and controlled by this.

He had tried various diets, cutting this out and adding this, to see if this would improve the pain and wind. Some days, this made a difference, but the next day, he would be back to square one. Nothing seemed to help. The only thing that he could link it to was the arrival of his sister back to his territory and the death of his parents. The sadness and fear of never seeing his parents again left him feeling unhappy. He now had more responsibility. He had to look out for his sister. He felt accountably for his sister, which made him feel even more fearful. Until then, he had been able to manage the pain and the wind and the occasional run to the toilet, but things were getting worse.

He then remembered this story he had once heard: It was a story about how heavy your glass is.

A teacher walked into her classroom and raised her glass of water. The students were thinking that she was going to ask the "half empty, or half full" question. Instead, with a smile on her face, she inquired: "How heavy is this glass of water?" Answers rang out.

She replied, "The absolute weight doesn't matter. It depends on how long I hold it. If I hold it for a minute, it's not a problem. If I hold it for an hour, I'll have an ache in my arm. If I hold it for a day, my arm will feel numb and paralyzed. In each case, the weight of the glass doesn't change, but the longer I hold it, the heavier it becomes." She continued, "The stresses and worries in life are like that glass of water. Think about them for a while, and nothing happens. Think about them a bit longer, and they begin to hurt. And if you think about them all day long, you will feel paralyzed – incapable of doing anything." It's important to remember to let go of your stresses. As early in the evening as you can, put all your burdens down. Don't carry them through the evening and into the night. Remember to put the glass down!

And so on this beautiful spring morning, this made the bear think and awaken to what he was holding onto, what he feared of letting go, and what was he holding onto from the past.

He began to repeat to himself. I release that which I no longer need. I now choose to seek new opportunities and fearlessly face the future.

The past is over, and I am free. It is the fear that is smothering me and I now choose to release that which I no longer need. The past is over, and I am free.

As the spring sun began to warm his body, the beautiful healing rays of golden light spread all over his body, allowing the tension, fear, sadness, guilt, and worry to be released.

He repeated: I easily release that which I no longer need. The past is over, and I am free. I forgive myself, and I forgive all who were involved, each and every one of them. The past is history. I freely and easily release the old and joyously welcome the new. As he stood there bathed in the beautiful rays of the sun, he could feel himself releasing and letting go of the burdens he was holding onto. He knew that he was enough just as he was. I am enough. I am enough.

Because all of these things began to happen just as he thought about them, he began to notice that he no longer worried the same. He no longer dwelled on things that would have caused him stress and strain, and he began to see things more clearly with more self-awareness and clarity without magnifying his own difficulties.

This made him think about the river that flowed beyond the meadow and how a river meanders throughout the countryside never worrying what's up ahead nor what it has just past. It continues smoothly on its journey without haste and without worry about what it will encounter. It lives in the now. When a river encounters a difficulty, it finds a new way around. It finds alternative solutions to solve that dilemma.

It doesn't dwell on the past or speculate on the future. Your unconscious mind is like that river able to find alternative answers; resources to any problems that you may encounter; so that it can overcome the negative, dark, and confusion. It's important to find new options, new choices, and new ways of being to overcome that issues.

When it feels like there is no path to follow, we go within to discover our deepest resources, and the light of inner knowing and intuition aids us in finding our way out of the darkness into the light. Go within now. Find your inner knowing, go within now.

THE PINK ROOM

(Learning to love and support yourself)

As you wander along, you notice a beautiful house in the distance, and there is something about this house that makes you stop and stare. You recognise this house, for it is the house that you have dreamt of the very night before, so the house feels very safe and secure.

You find yourself drawn along the path towards the front door. The gravel under your feet crunches as you come closer and closer to the entrance of the house. The front door is pink, just as you remembered it in your dream, and hope now springs forth in your mind that new understandings will be given and received.

You now open the door and enter the hall, you travel along the hall and turn right and you are now facing another pink door. You feel so safe and secure as you enter this room. Every area in this room is packed with beautiful pink bubbles. These bubbles are everywhere. Some are round, some are oval-shaped, and some are heart-shaped. There were small bubbles, medium bubbles, and large bubbles, all floating around the room.

These bubbles are now surrounding you, touching and tickling your nose, your face making you laugh and smile. You are feeling so happy, loved, nurtured, calm, and contented. The bubbles are now surrounding your whole body, and your whole body feels relaxed, loved, calm, and contented. These bubbles are now attached to your body, healing and rejuvenating, nurturing every cell in your body. Every cell in your body is now communicating with one another, sending and receiving beautiful loving happy information, each cell filling with love. You are now enveloped in unconditional love, and your heart fills with this divine energy. And it is within this energy that you hear the words: *I am love, I am contented, I am nurtured and respected. I completely love and respect myself so much so I make sure I fuel my body with loving, supporting food, and drink and with loving supporting thoughts.*

Even though I had an authority figure in my life who never showed any love or nurture, I now choose to love and accept my lack of nurturing away. I choose to love myself completely, deeply and profoundly.

I choose to say only loving, supportive, and accepting things to myself, and my actions demonstrate that I love and accept myself.

Raise your energy by accepting all of you the good and the bad bits. Also accept others for what they are. Relax and allow them to be who they are because when you respect yourself you can let go and just be.

As you relax and allow yourself to just be, there may be guilt, sadness, anger, and disappointment that you may need to release, because it is now safe to do so. Just above your head, you notice a large pink bubble, and you can forgive or free these emotions that no longer serve you. As you clear and empty your head, you will now feel lighter and lighter. You have let go of that which no longer serves you; these burdens that you have carried with you for such a long time, can go now never to return to you. Letting go, letting go, letting go.

You can see that pink bubble turning darker and darker and larger and larger as it absorbs and retains all of your troubles and worries. You now open the window in the room, freeing the bubble and liberating yourself. You watch the bubble floating into the sky, higher and higher; with it goes all of your pain and distress, leaving you to feel lighter and carefree.

Feeling happy, joyful, and lighter, you leave the room knowing that change has begun now, or later that day, as you begin and continue to use a new self-awareness, to be the person you so wish to be. And so it shall be.

THE SNAKE THAT LOST HER HISS

(Fear of speaking in public or speaking up for yourself)

This is a story about a snake. She was a lovely golden-coloured rattlesnake with gold and white markings all over her body. She lived in the jungle with her friends, slithering along the jungle floor, coiling around tree branches, and enjoying basking in the sunlight. Life was agreeable and worthwhile; she had a clear sense of direction and felt safe and secure.

One day, however, things changed for this beautiful snake when she awoke to find that she could no longer hiss. She breathed in as normal and expelled the air out through her throat, but no hiss came. She tried and tried to no avail. She needed to be able to do this to survive: to defend herself and intimidate predators from attacking her. She spoke with her friends who were really unsupportive and thought that the whole situation was highly amusing. She began to feel hopeless, ineffective, and powerless. She felt disconnected with her surroundings, unclear of how to move forward, out of balance, and unable to express her needs. She no longer felt safe and secure; she felt worried and unhappy, fearful that something terrible was about to happen. She felt under threat and in danger.

Weeks went by, and things remained the same. She worried about everything, the slightest noise making her jumpy and scared. She felt vulnerable and unable to protect herself. She felt powerless and defenceless, unable to defend her territory, incapable of expressing her worth and personal feelings. She decided that it was time to go and speak with the wise one of the jungle to seek advice and answers.

The snake explained to the wise one about her difficulties, worries, and fears. How powerless she felt, incapable of doing and being who she wished to be. The wise one explained that everyone has the ability to change and that there is always choice. Sometimes, we can see no other way of being. However, when we take a step back and observe, we can see things objectively. When you take a step back, your intentions become clearer, and it's within this clarity you realise which direction you need to strike out in. It will feel safe to make these changes, and there is no need to fear them.

Snakes have the ability to shed their own skin. As you shed your old skin, you can shed your illusions and limitations. And as you remove these illusions and limitations, you will then be able to use your energy and desires to achieve wholeness. You have the ability to shed old beliefs and habits that you have outgrown, moving into a higher energy and wisdom. This will bring balance and allow your mind to open to new possibilities. As you release the old, you can metamorphose into a new being, transforming, renewing, and healing. This creates and generates new knowledge and wisdom that will increase your energy and desires to achieve wholeness.

The snake then slithered back to her friends, feeling better and lighter, and soon she began to shed her skin, releasing the old emotions and freeing those self-limiting beliefs that were preventing her from transforming into something bigger and better. She visualised herself hissing louder and clearer, making her intentions known, feeling safe and secure enough to do this. Understanding that change is learning to trust and believe and knowing that its fear that keeps you quiet. She affirmed that she wanted to be heard and what she had to say was worthy and important. She stated this daily, making this her new belief, that she wanted to be heard. She needed to speak her truth and let others know.

So with every day that passed, her hiss became stronger and more powerful. She felt happier, confident, safe, and secure.

19

THE RACE OF LIFE

(Overcoming life's hurdles)

You are standing at the starting line. You are so full of excitement; your intentions goals and dreams are forefront in your mind, and you can see the winning post in the distance. (Think about what goals or dreams, and allow yourself to see and what you wish to achieve.) You can see this, feel it, and hear how this will be. The red ribbons wait for you to run through them as your sweet prize is realised and achieved.

You are like a new-born lamb; you feel light. You're skipping around and jumping. Everything is new fresh and so exciting. You can see your ambitions and dreams unfolding. You are focused on what you want to achieve. (Reaffirm what you wish to achieve.)

You start on your journey, full of promise motivation and drive, moving swiftly towards the winning line. Obstacles appear that begin to slow you down. You run across what you thought was sand, but this turns out to be sinking sand. The first few steps are fine, and you find yourself sinking deeper and deeper into the wet sand. The more you struggle, the more you find yourself stuck. Your frantic movements cause you to become even more lodged. You feel trapped, certain that you will not succeed. It feels like you're on an obstacle course. The first hurdles you come across show your dreams floating past. That winning post is so far in the distance it looks like a dot in the background and this makes you feel even more withdrawn and stuck.

So you take a moment to gather your thoughts and slow your frantic movements and to stop yourself from getting stuck deeper. And you find yourself relaxing and taking your time developing patience. Because you now find yourself relaxing, you are now able to see things clearly and in their true perceptive. You can now find original solutions to overcome this problem. By relaxing, calming the mind, and breathing slowly, you find that the more you spread out your weight, the harder it will be to sink even deeper. Relaxation is key because when you relax the mind, new answers become available to solve and work out any troubles. You ask your unconscious mind to help solve the problem that is preventing you from achieving your dreams. So you find yourself relaxing in the quick sand and bending backwards, and this allows your legs to become free. You begin to sweep your arms backwards as if you were swimming, and this propels you to firm ground.

Now that you are back on firm ground, you can again see your prize and desires. And so you continue on your journey, feeling stronger and more focused. You find yourself moving quickly and easily towards your goals. As you continue along your path, a second hurdle presents itself. There is a deep, steep-sided river valley that no longer has a river flowing through it.

It appears that the only way across this valley is on a tightrope. The tightrope is strung tightly between two positions, high above the ground. There is a pole to also help you balance across this valley.

This pole represents your personal life/work balance. You place the pole in your hand with your feet still firmly on solid ground, and you find that the pole is now swinging to the right towards work and then to the left towards family. The pole needs to remain centred, focused, and balanced for our achievements to become attainable. So what needs to be balanced in your life? What adjustments do you need to make in your world? As you contemplate the pole in your hand, you can now see what has been out of balance and how important it is to have life in an equal, peaceful harmonious path. Your path has been torn between family commitments and work projects, and your dreams have become forgotten. Because your dreams have become forgotten, you have found that there is a void, an emptiness within you, just like the valley below. So thinking about yourself: By being self-fulfilled, that void can be replenished with love and hope. You are now one and, the pole becomes balanced and focused once more on your dreams. It's while you are holding the pole straight and centred that you notice a golden bridge. Still holding the pole, as this is a reminder of balance, you cross the bridge safely to the opposite side of the valley.

You can now see the winning post ahead. You have nearly reached your destination. Wow! What a journey this has been. You run through the ribbons now and hold up the golden trophy. You are victorious. Well done, well done. You sit for a moment and contemplate the obstacles that you have overcome on this journey. You remember how you had been stuck, not knowing where or how to move forward. You recall being out of balance, overlooking and disconnecting from your purpose and mission. As you overcame these hurdles with self-belief, love, and inner strength, you were able to continue towards your finishing line, achieving your wishes and desires.

You were focused on your dreams, reaffirming them daily while visualising and manifesting. Most importantly, you also learned to detach yourself from the outcome, knowing that these seeds or dreams you had planted were growing and flourishing daily. You never dig up these seeds to see how far they had developed. You nourished, trusted, and believed that they would grow and bloom into the vision you had created in your mind. This allowed you to go with the flow of life to experience new directions and changes even greater than you had ever dreamt of.

MAGICAL GARDEN

(To assist with balance, self-confidence, and self-esteem)

This is a story about a woman called Minnie who had a real passion for life. She enjoyed supporting and motivating people to get the greatest good from them so that they could achieve their fullest potential.

Sometimes, however, she was met with so much resistance from the people she was trying to help that it felt as though she were stuck in quicksand or trying to wade through a river in full flood, the water gushing towards her, knocking her down, and preventing her from moving forward.

It was these people who she found the greatest challenge, those whose flaws she could see quite clearly. Although she felt it was for their greatest good to make them aware of this, these individuals continued to do the exact thing that she had so kindly made them aware of.

In a work environment, it was easy to find an answer. When it came to friends, relatives, and acquaintances, she found this really baffling to deal with. People would sulk or brood for days before eventually speaking to her once again. And then they would continue just as they had been, taking no heed of her advice or guidance. This caused her to feel so frustrated and unhappy with them that they did not want to improve and develop themselves. She began to think about whether she really needed to maintain this friendship or attachment. She would ponder over their positive qualities and the memories and fun they had together. However, these characteristics she felt needed improvement were still not being rectified. She felt that their friendship was no longer on the same footing or balance.

It was this problem she was thinking about when she out walking, when she came across a small gate with a beautiful arch over the top of it, draped in beautiful honeysuckle. The honeysuckle had wrapped itself all around the arch, and the sweet-smelling flowers provided a powerful and intoxicating scent. Minnie stood there for several moments enjoying the fragrance, and peacefulness swept over her. She wandered through a gate that led her into a beautiful garden. She paused for a moment, observing the lovely and glorious scene that unfolded in front of her. The colours were amazing pinks, violets, purples, blues, orange, greens, and reds — all the colours of the rainbow.

She was now in a stunning meadow, the flowers with their various hues creating a mosaic so incredible that it left Minnie speechless. She became aware that the flowers were all floating just above her head, moving in the breeze as with they were dancing to an unheard melody. It reminded Minnie of the colourful flower shaped windmills she used to hold as a child. She used to blow on the windmill, the colours dancing, moving and turning in the sunlight. She tried to jump up to catch some of these dancing flowers; however, they always remained just outside her reach, her hands brushing only against the stems. The flowers would laugh, and their flower heads would circle a little faster, swaying in the warm breeze.

She wandered across the meadow, and her eye caught a light green patch of grass. There were several of these patches throughout the meadow, and when her feet touched this light green patch, it was bouncy like a trampoline. She found herself bouncing up and down on the grass, which propelled her higher and higher into the sky. As she jumped, she was able to catch the flowers. As she jumped, she laughed and giggled with joy. It was fun trying to catch the different colours of flowers as they floated around the meadow.

She had now six coloured flowers (indigo, violet, orange, blue, yellow, and red) in her hand. She had one final flower to collect (the green one), and as she clasped this flower, she found herself being lifted into the air by the flowers. The colour green represents peace and harmony and creates clarity and freedom within all situations. The flowers' heads all moved in continuous circles, all flowing at the same speed and all in balance. This enabled Millie to drift safely and securely above the meadow.

As Minnie drifted above the meadow, she could see things so differently from how she did before. She had a clearer perspective, and she could see things from an objective point of view. People had free will and choice, and if they choose not to have this new awareness, that was their decision. Perhaps in the future, they may feel differently and want to attempt or experiment with change to overcome whatever issues they have. Minnie now had a new awareness that she had to accept people as they are. She had to learn to accept them and not the behaviours that upset her. She drifted around the meadow, pondering and thinking about this new understanding she had. She contemplated how this would be for her. Could accepting people as they are be the answer she was looking for? As she drifted back down into the meadow, she released the flowers, freeing them to soar and drift to new spaces and places.

As Minnie wandered back towards the gate, she discovered a light-green chameleon basking in the sun. This animal can adapt to its environment, when it is happy or contented, it turns more of a light-green. What message was the chameleon bringing? The chameleon was reaffirming about balance and blending in with the circumstances. With this new acceptance, she decided to adapt to her own environment and surroundings. She had to allow and accept that people had free will and can change only when they feel the time is right, and she had to have patience and lead by example.

21

CHAINED TO THE PAST

(Letting go of old beliefs that no longer serve your highest worth)

You are in your house. You feel safe and secure, comfortable being here. You wander through to the rear of the house, and you look around the room that you have entered. You notice something that you have never seen before. There appears to be a wall that's surface is different from the other three walls. You move closer to inspect this wall and discover that right in the centre of the wall is an indentation. You push this part of the wall, and when you do so, the entire panel of wall moves inwards, revealing a secret passage. You decide to investigate to see where this passage leads. The passage expands into a huge room, and in the centre of this room sits a huge treasure chest. The treasure chest is made of dark brown wood and finely finished with a round top. On the round top of the chest, there is a picture of a ship with three masts and sails. There is also an image of a fish leaping in the air. The chest has big brass hinges and locks and smells of the sea. The treasure chest is bound with three steel-linked chains and a lock. The lock is a combination lock and requires three numbers to release the chains, one number for each chain.

You look at the chest, and it makes you speculate about what might be inside this beautiful chest. You are curious about what treasures lie within, that remain hidden, and what prizes await discovery. These chains prevent you from discovering what is within. You touch the heavy chains, and they clink and clank against the treasure chest. You think about the fortune that might lie within: gold and silver jewels, money, or gold coins. You start to dream about how this would change your life and how much happier you would be. You dream of a large house, fast cars, and all the beautiful things that you would buy. You could have anything your heart desired. First, though, you needed to unlock the lock to free the chains preventing you from attaining your goal.

It made you then think about what chains you had bound around yourself, preventing you from moving forward and achieving your own treasure or fortune.

There were three main chains:

(1) The chain of self-belief
(2) The chain of trust
(3) The chain of speaking your truth

What would it mean to you to have those chains removed?
How would your life change if those chains were gone?
What do you need to say that would allow you to feel fulfilled?

You sit and ponder on those chains; you wonder what self-limiting beliefs you are holding onto that no longer serve your best interests. What beliefs prevent you from accomplishing your dreams? Whom do you need to trust, and what do you need to say to yourself or others to become true to yourself?

You realise that you are like the treasure chest and that what you seek lies within. All the knowledge, skills, awareness, and resources are there inside of you to utilise. You are the one who has created the chains of limitation, but you are also the one who can uproot and eliminate these shackles. Be like the ship engraved on the treasure chest that encourage us to navigate whatever rough seas are present, so we can experience the journey of life. The fish represents flowing with life, wealth, prosperity, and success, as well as a clearer understanding of the self.

So it's time now to remove the chains you have created, so that you can now attract self-belief, trust, and abundance that you so desire.

So you look at the padlock, and you choose the first number:

You choose the number three since it represents the total of the chains that binds you and the treasure chest.

The second number you choose is the number eight, the number that represents infinity, limitless power, and strength.

The third number you choose is number two, which signifies balance, understanding, and trust.

As you turn the combination lock to 382, the first chain releases and falls with a clatter to the floor. The second chain frees itself from the chest and smashes to the floor. The third chain resists, but with faith, trust, and courage, it too relaxes and surrenders. With each chain that is released, you can feel yourself becoming lighter and freer. Those burdens you have been carrying around are now gone. Those burdens you were carrying are now gone for good. You now turn and open the treasure chest, and it contains your heart's desire, your dreams, and your wishes, as well as truth and hope. You have opened your chest and set yourself free.

22

BEE LIKE THE LOTUS FLOWER

(Overcoming diversity to achieve what you desire)

You are wandering through a garden it's a beautiful sunny day, and the birds are singing. Their tunes light and full of promise. The bees are buzzing flying from one flower to the next. The bee's body shakes in a certain way to get the pollen off of the flower. The buzzing sounds caused by the vibration of its wings, which beat up to 200 times a second as it moves from plant to plant pollinating, play a delicate role in the balance of our ecosystem.

There are those special bees that serve as honey producers, delivering that magically sweet nectar to us. Honey is an elixir of life with many healing properties; it stimulates the growth of new cells and tissues and speeds up the healing process. Its honeycomb, a hexagon, is the symbol of the heart and represents the sweetness of life found within our own heart.

Bees coexist in harmony and live as a unit within the hive. Each insect has a job to do that serves the greater good. Each individual contributes to the survival and success of the group. This demonstrates the power of community and teamwork, therefore allowing them to prosper in their endeavours.

You begin to think about this insect and how it shouldn't be able to fly. Its body is too large for its wings. It's a symbol that anything is possible. By putting your mind to it, you can accomplish anything. No matter how great the vision is, there is the promise of fulfilment if we pursue our dreams.

It prompts you to examine what has been going on in your life. Perhaps this is a message from the powerful yet humble bee. Have you been a busy bee lately? Perhaps you are devoting too much time to work and not enough time to play. It's important to remember the sweetness in life. Even all the hard work of the bee results in the satisfaction of rich honey. The bee's message could also be one of teamwork and community. Are you being called to raise the vibration of the world and make it a better place to live?

The bee flies off and lands on a beautiful white lotus flower. The flower's roots are firmly embedded in the mud of the water where it grows. It emerges as pure white from the depths of the muddy swamp and grows above the water. Its petals open one by one. When night falls, the lotus flower closes and goes beneath the water. At dawn, it climbs above the water and reopens. The lotus flower is the symbol of transformation from darkness into the light, creation and rebirth, and from innocence into wisdom towards peace and serenity.

You now can contemplate and review this flower's meaning in order to grow and gain wisdom. First, you must have the mud. The mud represents the suffering and obstacles in life. Every human shares the same hurdles: sadness, loss, illness, dying, and death. This suffering is a vital part in the human experience;

it makes us stronger and teaches us to resist the temptation of evil. When we banish evil thoughts from our minds, we are able to break free of the muddy water. With more kindness and compassion, we then have the intention to grow as a lotus flower, and open each petal one by one. Even in the darkest days, we know that light will follow. The mud shows us who we are and teaches us to choose the right path over the easy one.

So we have a lot to learn from the lotus flower. Through suffering, we can grow and develop and journey from the darkness into the light. From the bee, we can learn that despite the impracticality of the bee's aerodynamics, it's still able to fly.

7504512R00086

Printed in Great Britain
by Amazon.co.uk, Ltd.,
Marston Gate.